Candle Making at Home

A User-Friendly Beginner's Guide

Kelley Shavonne Norris

Copyright 2021 © Kelley Shavonne Norris

All Rights Reserved

Table of Contents

Introduction 4
Chapter 1- Safety Precautions 5
Chapter 2: What Are Candles? 9
Chapter 3- Tools and Equipment Necessary 23
Chapter 4- Using Essential Oils 34
Chapter 5- Coloring Candles 43
Chapter 6- The Fundamentals of Candle Making 51
Chapter 7- 35 Simple Candle Recipes... 67
Chapter 8- 6 Common Candle Making Errors 85
Chapter 9- Diagnosing and Fixing Any Problems 88
Chapter 10- Decorating and Storing Your Candles 93

Introduction

Everybody needs a bit of light to brighten up their lives, and what better way to do that than by making your own homemade candles. Now don't be shy; creating new things is an exhilarating process, and it is one you will surely appreciate as you go along. Homemade products are underrated, and candles can shine new light on that dreary space, transforming it into a haven of warmth and comfort.

However, like most things in life, candles won't last forever. But you are learning the ins and outs of candle making, and as such, you will be able to create an infinite amount of candles with the same amount of possibilities. In this book, you will learn all about tools, equipment, safety guidelines, 35 recipes, and so much more, all conveniently together in one place. So don't get stuck in the dark when you can create your own light; that just so happens to smell great too.

Chapter 1- Safety Precautions

Your safety should always be your main concern when undertaking a new project, and as such, you should make sure that you are adequately protected and prepared before you start. By following these safety precautions and wearing your protective equipment, you can drastically minimize the likelihood of causing harm to yourself or others around you during your candle-making journey.

Have safety equipment on hand

As a beginner, you will become all too familiar with spills, and even the most experienced candle-maker is bound to have an accident or two. This is why you will need perseverance and patience. These two things will be your key to success along your journey through candle-making. Mistakes can happen at any time, and because of this, you will need to make sure that you are well equipped should anything go wrong. By wearing your protective equipment and adhering to safety protocols, you can significantly reduce the chance of damage befalling you or anyone else.

However, even if you are using safety equipment and wearing protective gear, you will need a plan "B" should any such scenario arise. You can use water and a cloth to wipe up any simple wax spills (it will need to be hot water if the wax has already hardened). Additionally, you should also purchase a fire extinguisher or candle snuffer to manage any wax fires, and always remember never to use water to put out a wax fire as it can cause the wax to splatter.

Use the correct tool and equipment and follow your recipe.

Having the right tools, equipment, and recipe for the job is always essential for getting the project right. With just about everything now available online, it is crucial to get your recipe from a trusted source, as this will prevent any problems from arising unnecessarily during your journey. Similarly speaking, making sure you are also using the correct tools and equipment for candle making is also crucial.

However, these tools will be covered later on in a future chapter, explaining precisely what you will need for the candle-making process. Lastly, to ensure that you don't confuse any candle-making utensils with household ones, I recommend labeling them to ensure that your tools never get mixed up.

Keep children and animals away from your workspace.

This step is crucial as you will be working with flammable substances and potent essential oils or chemical additives. Having pets or children wandering around your workspace can be incredibly dangerous and can lead to severe or life-threatening injuries. Therefore, you must ensure that pets and children stay out of your workspace at all times unless accompanied by a responsible adult.

Ensure a clean and well-organized workspace

Before you begin creating something new, you will need to ensure that your space is clean and well organized. By making sure that your room is free of clutter, you can prevent unnecessary spills or accidents, as you will be able to freely move around your workspace while you are making your candles. This will help to lessen any chance of bodily harm coming to you or others nearby.

Keep your workspace well ventilated.

A significant risk that is often overlooked when it comes to candle making is working with wax and essential oils. Inhaling the fumes caused by melting wax as well as adding in essential oils can cause mild to severe bodily harm, depending on how much you take in. You should always try to wear a protective mask or purchase a ventilator, and you should never work in a poorly ventilated area. You must always make sure that your workstation has at least one window and it remains open while you are working and when your candles are setting once completed.

Have all your components ready beforehand

Making candles is a simple and relatively easy process. However, this process can be made even simpler by ensuring that you have all your tools, equipment, recipe, and ingredients ready and waiting before you begin. By doing this, you will have everything you need nearby, enabling your candle-making to go ahead smoothly without a hitch. Candle-making is a relatively quick process, so time is of the essence, so make sure that you are well prepared before you begin.

Protect your eyes

Looking at safety protocols, when it comes to your eyes, protecting them should be your number one priority. When working with wax, there are many scenarios where something can go wrong, like backsplashes while you are in the middle of candle making. This scenario could end up harming your eyes. Luckily for you, a quick and easy fix is readily available to you, known as safety goggles or glasses. This one item can reduce and just about guarantee your eyes remain protected and out of harm's way.

Protect your skin

Your skin is just as susceptible to burns and damage from hot wax as your eyes are. If you are not wearing protective equipment like rubber or latex gloves, with long sleeves to match, the hot wax can come into contact with your skin, and as a result, you can be burned. Specifically speaking, when it comes down to skin protection, you shouldn't be taking it lightly and should always use some form of coverage as protection for your skin.

Using wax

When trying new things for the first time, there are bound to be risks involved; this is especially true for beginners new to candle-making. Always remember that wax is a flammable substance and should be handled with caution and never left unattended, as it can result in irreparable damage to you or your property through fire. Additionally, when working with wax, you are bound to have some splashback, and as such, you should be wearing your safety gear, i.e., your goggles and gloves, to prevent exposure to your skin and eyes. Moreover, you should also be wearing your mask and or using a ventilator to ensure that you are not risking exposure to the toxic fumes.

Record your processes

When you have created your first batch of candles, recording your results as you go through the process will be highly beneficial for you. By doing this, you will be able to check back over past recipes and see if there was anything you might have left out, have to add in, or if something has gone wrong.

Recording your actions and process can help you to prevent the same problems from occurring in future projects. That being said, once you become more confident in your candle-making abilities, you will also begin to learn how to customize your own candle recipes to your specific looks, wants, and needs.

Chapter 2: What Are Candles?

Candles are amongst some of the earliest inventions in our world, with evidence of candlesticks present in Crete and Egypt from as far back as 3000 BC. So what is a candle, you may be wondering? Well, a candle can come in varying shapes, sizes, colors, and waxes and can consist of varying types of wicks that are submerged in either wax, tallow, or gel as its fuel source. Combined with colors and or fragrances, candles can turn a dark and depressing space into one that oozes light and warmth.

What is a candle?

Candles can be made with varying types of waxes, and depending on the type of wax you use will depend on the kind of candle you will be making. There are many different varieties of candles from a pillar, taper/dinner, scented, decorative, and tea light candles to flameless, votive, birthday, candle pot, and more. Each comes with its own function and setting depending on the space and what you are using or looking for. You can purchase these varieties at your local store or online through a retailer. Otherwise, you can try your luck making them at home.

Candle varieties

Pillar candles- These wax candles are designed to be harder and denser than container wax candle types. A pillar candle is cylindrical and is molded from wax that is hard enough to retain its shape while burning. You may be wondering, well, what could be so great about a harder wax? Well, a denser wax automatically means a harder candle and as such, removing these candles from molds is a breeze. Therefore pillar wax is ideal for creating wax melts and pillar candles.

Taper/dinner candles- These are tall and thin and are designed explicitly for candelabras and candlesticks.

Scented candles- These candles are ideal for bringing your home to life with aromatherapy and are made up of scent notes categorized into three levels, top, middle, and base.

Unscented- If you love the aesthetic that comes with candles, but you just can't stand to be near one because the smell is overbearing, then these unscented candles will be ideal for you. They are perfect for dinners or events where you simply want to appreciate the aromas of your meal or enjoy the moment without your allergies popping up. Functional and attractive unscented candles still get the job done, whether at home or work.

Decorative candles- These candles never fail in delivering beauty to the heart of your home or space by shaping the room's style. These kinds of candles are perfect for table centerpieces, dining tables, bookshelves, and many many more areas of your home or office.

Tea light candles- The smallest among candle varieties at just 0.63 inches/0.7cm tall and 1.5 inches/3.8cm wide, these candles are cheap and offer you the most aesthetic when placed in groups on high or low surfaces.

Flameless- These artificial candles have become increasingly popular in recent years because they are long-lasting without the fire hazard. These types of candles require batteries or a charging cable, and you won't need to worry about leaving them unattended, being burned, or producing any smoke. But they will still give your space that warm and inviting atmosphere without worrying about it being a stagnant light source as flameless candles are designed to mimic the natural flicker of candlelight.

Votive- Classified as a relatively small candle sitting at just 2.5 inches/6.3cm tall and two inches/5cm wide, these votive candles are still bigger than tea-light candles. These types of candles produce no smoke making them popular for the indoors. Additionally, votive candles need to be set in a flame retardant container so you won't have to stress about safety and flame control. Moreover, once your votive candle has burned to the base, it will simply smother itself out, meaning you won't have to watch these candles like a hawk worrying about a fire starting.

Candle pot- These candles are poured directly into a glass jar, pot, or tin container, and because of this, they won't shift or become dislodged from their mold. As a result, these candles are perfect for your home or office as they come with their own lid ensuring your scent remains strong when in storage, and any wax melts directly into the container for a no-mess, no-fuss approach.

Birthday- You would recognize this candle at first sight from any birthday as they come in copious bold and bright colors. They are crucial for use on birthday cakes as they light quickly to ensure that no wax runs down the candle onto the cake. Additionally, birthday candles can also come as gimmicks where the candle doesn't blow out or looks like a sparkler when lit.

Floating- These candles are a great way to incorporate tranquil beauty with safety as floating candles sit on top of a body of water when used. As such, you won't have to worry about any wax spills getting onto your surfaces or the candles being knocked over as they are in the water. Like tea-light candles, they are small in size and tend to burn down in a few hours instead of larger, regular candles.

Tarts- Making candles without the wick is possible if you use wax tarts, also known as wax melts. Melting the wax tarts or melts using a tart burner or potpourri opens up a whole new world of enjoying scented candles without the wick or flame: all this plus the added benefit of being able to use natural or artificial wax to make them.

Container candles- These types of candles are specifically designed to sit within a glass container, jar, or metal tin, either with or without a lid. These candles cannot stand on their own and are often made from softer wax types like soy, paraffin blends, paraffin, and palm wax. Additionally, container candles can also be made from beeswax but will require a larger or multiple wicks to burn properly. Moreover, if your wax doesn't stick flush to the sides of your container, you could end up having a candle that looks like it has wax spots. While this could be a possibility for your container candles, it is more often the reality when you use pillar waxes inside a container. These container waxes can come in an array of types like slab, granulated, and even in flake form.

Gel candles- This type of candle doesn't use wax; instead, it uses a mineral oil-based gel poured into a heat-proof container to form a candle with the same consistency as gelatin. This wax can be used in container candles but will require your fragrances to be incorporated into your wax at 170F/76C. Moreover, you will need to dilute your fragrance or essential oils in a ratio of 50% fragrance to 50% mineral oil.

Rolled candles- These candles are made using rollable sheets of wax with a wick in the center and are some of the most common candles because of their simplicity. They are made with beeswax and come in sheets of 8inches by 16 inches/20cm by 40cm and are eco-friendly as well as being easy and safe to use.

Dipped candles- As the name suggests, dipped candles are exactly that. These candles are primed wicks, submerged in multiple layers of wax to build up different colors and shades until a whole candle has formed.

Types of candle wax

Natural waxes

Candle wax can be natural or artificial in nature, and as a candle maker, you will need to understand the main differences between the two. Natural wax is biodegradable, sustainable, burns for a longer time than artificial waxes, and is easier to clean up. Unfortunately, these natural waxes can be hard to find even at your DIY or arts and crafts stores, so purchasing them online is going to be your best bet at acquiring these natural waxes.

Soybean wax

Made from soybean oil, soy wax is both renewable and natural, meaning it is the best choice as a sustainable wax for candle-makers. Soybeans are naturally biodegradable and provide a long and clean burn for your candle. Additionally, soy wax is excellent as you won't have a hard time cleaning up any spills off surfaces, as all it takes is a bit of hot water and a cloth.

- 100% natural
- Cost affordable
- It comes in various blends with or without additives that can be purchased online or at your local arts and crafts or DIY store.
- As long as your blend of wax is listed at or above 51%, it will be a soy wax blend.
- It should only be used for container candles as it is too soft for other projects like tarts.
- The candle maker can use it in other candles if stearic acid is added to the wax to make it stronger.

Bayberry wax

This type of wax comes from berries that are found on the Bayberry bush. These berries are harvested and then boiled to create the sage-green colored wax known for its spicy fragrance. Unfortunately, this wax will cost you quite a pretty penny, so unless you are confident in your skills, it is best to avoid using this wax as a beginner as it will prevent a costly mistake.

- Expensive
- Known for its spicy aroma and green-colored wax.
- It can be used in container candles.

Beeswax

Straight out of nature's garden, this wax is stickier than any other wax available and is renowned amongst candle-makers for its ability to burn consistently. Moreover, this type of wax will require a thicker wick size to burn well.

- Natural sweet fragrance
- You can purchase it in slabs, blocks, pre-rolled sheets, or pastilles
- Costly to purchase
- The candle maker can use it in container candles

Important note: There are a few other natural waxes that you can substitute with these listed above, such as palm wax (can be used in container candles), coconut wax, and jojoba wax.

Artificial waxes

Paraffin wax

As the most inexpensive type of wax, paraffin wax is also the most predominant kind available on the market today and is made from crude oil that has been excessively refined. It is typically used in commercial candles and generally leaves behind a lot more soot than other wax types and is generally not favored amongst natural candle-makers.

- The most common option for candle making
- It is made through refining crude oil
- Not necessarily toxic
- Readily available
- Harder and more brittle than natural wax
- Lower oil content, higher melting point, faster burn
- The candle maker can use it in container candles

Gel wax

Gel wax is ideal for candle making because of its visual appeal and melt and pour potential. This type of wax is manufactured from mineral oil mixed with thermoplastic resin and butylated hydroxytoluene. This means it is not suited for aromatherapy candles. Additionally, gel wax is incompatible when mixed with natural essential oils as it is an artificial wax.

- See-through
- Will typically perform as standard waxes do
- It is now available for use in pillar candles
- The candle maker can use it in container candles

Granulated and melt and pour waxes

Granulated waxes

Granulated waxes are often used for craft projects because of how easy they are to use. They are made from 140F/60C melt-point paraffin, which has been manufactured into small beads which you can simply pour into a container with the wick inserted without the need to heat the wax.

Melt and pour waxes

Candle wax, like soaps, can also come in melt and pour varieties like pre-scented soy wax varieties, which you can purchase online or at your local arts and crafts or DIY store. These melt and pour waxes need only be heated and poured. You can do this once the wax has cooled to 70F/21C before pouring it into your container with your wick. Additionally, these waxes can come in varying blends depending on the company you are sourcing your wax from, so be sure to do some research before purchasing a specific one.

Wax additives

Wax additives come in a wide variety to fix a multitude of candle-making problems. Some of these additives can increase candle flexibility and luster, help remove candles from their molds, and preserve the color. As the term additive suggests, these add-ins are artificial, and most candle-makers prefer to steer clear of them in favor of more natural options. However, most candles will be just fine without these added extras, but there could come a time when you might be facing a particular problem that only an additive can fix. Listed below are a few additives that are commonly used in candle making.

Luster crystals- These crystals provide a vibrant, almost cloudy sheen as well as a candle that will burn for longer. The recommended amount for candle making is 0.16oz/4.5g per 1lb/454g of wax.

Micro Crystallines- These are highly refined waxes that you will use to transform the properties of the carrier wax. Even though micro crystallines come in a wide range, they can be separated into two main types: pliable or durable. Pliability is used to make the candle more elastic for molding and maximize the wax's adherence ability. Durability is used to make your wax harder and stronger. However, adding more than 2% of micro crystallines into your batch can cause burning and wick problems.

Snow wax- This wax, when added to your carrier wax, must be done in such a way that the wax is melted down separately before being mixed. This will give your candles an iridescent and high gloss finish in addition to preventing the candle from sagging in hot weather. Additionally, it will also improve the length of time your candle burns and the overall surface texture. It is advised that snow wax be used as 0.16oz/4.5g per 1lb/454g of wax.

Snowflake oil- This oil is used when decorating, and as the name suggests, it creates an intricate snowflake design that you will see in standard aromatic commercial candles. When purchasing this item, you will need to follow the recommended instructions that come included.

Stearic acid- This acid is added to paraffin to improve the amount of time your candle will burn and give it a cloudy appearance. It is advised to use 0.3-0.8oz/8.5-22.6g per 1lb/454g of wax for use in candle making.

Vybar- This additive is used to strengthen, minimize shrinkage, fix the scent into the wax, and turn the candle an opaque color. To use this, it is advised that no more than 0.3oz/8.5g is added per 1lb/454g of wax.

Wax dyes

Specifically created to color candle wax, these dyes are chemically synthetic and are made using an oily chemical substrate known as anilines. They come in three distinct types, liquid, dye blocks, and flakes, which are water-soluble, all the while still producing a pleasing color for your candle. Liquid dyes provide potent colors, while flake and block dyes will give you more pale and pastel colors.

It is crucial to note that some fragrances and essential oils can possibly change the color of your finished candle, so be sure to check the ingredients, usage instructions, and caution or warning labels before you begin.

Types of candle wicks

In today's day and age, you will be able to find all types of candle wicks online or at your community arts and craft or DIY stores. Before selecting your wick, it is crucial to remember that you will need to do some experimentation to achieve the correct height and design of the wick for the candle you will be making. The wicks listed here are the four basic kinds and recommendations for each use but are not guaranteed as many variables factor in when it comes to choosing the proper wick type for your candle. These factors include fragrance load, container diameter, wax type, and the type of dye you will be using.

As with any new batch, you should always do a test burn to ensure that your wick is burning correctly. Most candle-makers prefer candle wicks that have already been pre-waxed as they are simpler to use overall and therefore much better for beginners to use. However, if you haven't primed wicks, you can do it at home by simply soaking your wick for five minutes in hot wax, then removing it to dry thoroughly on wax paper. Below are the four basic candle wicks that are typically used in candle making.

Wire-core wicks

- This type of wick is typically used more for containers, tea lights, and votive-style candles.
- It can sometimes come already pre-tabbed and only need to be stuck to the bottom of your mold, jar, or container.
- The metal core is often composed of zinc but can also be manufactured from lead in some instances and will be hazardous when burned.

Flat-braided wicks

- This type of wick is generally used in dipped or taper candles
- When used, the wick's v's should always be facing the top of the candle to prevent carbonized balls from forming on the top of your wick.

Square-braided

This type of wick is used in pillar candles as it is far sturdier than the flat-braided kind.

Paper-core wicks

- This type of wick is generally used in tea lights, containers, and votive candles.
- Tends to smoke more than other candle wicks

Sizing your wicks

When it comes to sizing your wick for your candle, some factors have to be considered. The diameter and length of your wick will usually be determined by the size of the candle that you will be making. Wick size will also be determined by the type of wax that you will use for your candle. Beeswax and paraffin that have had additives included will burn for a longer length of time and, as such, will require a larger-sized wick.

The diameter of the finished candle can determine the size of the wick; therefore, if your candle is two inches/5cm in diameter, you will use a small wick, which you can also use for votive candles. For a medium-sized wick, your candle will need to be between 2-3 inches/5-7.6cm in diameter, and for a large-sized wick, your candle will need to be between 3-4 inches/7.6-10.2cm in diameter.

Moreover, you can also determine the length of the wick by measuring the height of your candle mold and then adding two inches/5cm. You might want to leave a longer wick for decorative purposes as it can be knotted or embellished with items like charms or beads.

Important note: The most prevalent reason for a poorly burning candle is often the incorrect selection of the wick for the diameter of the candle or the wax from which it is made. To achieve the best consistency, it is crucial to always be recording your steps and the process you took to get there.

Candle molds

Molds for candles can come in endless varieties of sizes and shapes and can be manufactured from plastic, metal, rubber, or acrylic. Most are light on the wallet and can be recycled repeatedly once the original candle has been finished or repurposed. Not only can you use these bought containers, but you can also repurpose certain items that you find around your home for a greener approach to your project. These items can include things like eggshells, polished aluminum cans, that broken mug with no handle you were going to toss away, and mason jars, naming only a few.

Types of candle molds

Standard molds

Plastic mold- A favorite for newbies as they can be cheaply acquired while still being safe to handle. Additionally, these types of molds are easy to clean, only requiring a small amount of soap and water. Unfortunately, the downside of plastic olds is their tendency not to last very long.

Aluminum mold- This mold is one of the most common amongst candle makers for its heat-resistant ability, low maintenance, and long-lasting shelf life. Additionally, aluminum molds are relatively more cost-effective than those like rubber and won't cause seam lines to appear on your candle. Regrettably, the only problem with these kinds of molds is they have a limited variety of shapes and sizes and need a releasing agent to remove the candle from its mold.

Metal mold- Due to the high shelf life of metal molds, they have become increasingly popular because of their varying shapes and sizes, in addition to being easy to clean. Moreover, you won't have to worry about seam lines, and a metal mold will last you far longer than most other molds on the market.

Rubber molds

These molds can come in an array of categories, with some of them listed below.

Polyurethane mold- A cheaper alternative to actual rubber is polyurethane molds. It will often require a releasing agent to be added to your wax before the candle can be released from its mold quickly. Regrettably, these kinds of molds, although popular with mold makers, will give your candle a strange smell once finished.

Latex mold- Latex molds are typically designed with complex shapes like fruits, animals, or flowers, to name a few. These molds are highly flexible, and as such, you will have the freedom to create elaborate designs. Additionally, latex does not require any additives for mold release and is a popular option for its versatility.

Silicone mold- A popular choice of mold as it comes in various sizes and shapes, and because of its no-stick ability, you can easily remove your candles from these molds. With a flexible surface, you won't need any help from mold-releasing additives. However, regrettably, these molds will withhold scent, have mild instability and are usually quite expensive.

Glass mold- As one of the most popular molds in candle making for its ability to cool down your candle quickly, therefore saving you both time and money. Famous not just because they are time-saving but also because they don't require any mold releasing additives for you to remove your candle from the mold. Moreover, glass molds are readily available; however, the only disadvantages of these molds are the high fragility and weakness to prolonged exposure to heat and may explode due to repeated heating and cooling of the glass.

Important note: Specialised molds like seamless, votive, and pillar will have to be purchased from a reputable retailer.

To make your own easy candle mold, you can follow these simple instructions below to create a mold from corrugated cardboard.

Easy corrugated cardboard candle mold

Materials you will need

- Corrugated cardboard
- Box or duct tape
- A plastic lid larger than your mold
- Wick
- Mold sealer

Steps

1. To utilize this material, you will first need to pre-coat (with vegetable oil) the corrugated side of the cardboard.
2. With the now coated corrugated side of the cardboard facing inwards, you can now begin to shape your mold into either a square, round, or triangular as preferred.
3. Now that you have the shape you desire, you can use a box or duct tape to keep it from losing its shape.
4. Make a small hole using a needle in the center of the lid.
5. With the mold sealer, you can now secure your corrugated cardboard to the top of the lid. Make sure to center it around your pre-poked hole, leaving no gaps for leaks.

6. Thread the wick through the hole in the lid. You will have to seal it with a mold sealer around the outside of the mold to prevent any leaks.
7. Pour the wax into the mold. Once set, you can tear the cardboard away from the sides of the candle.

Chapter 3- Tools and Equipment Necessary

You will need these essential items to begin your candle-making journey but fret not, as you can find most of these items at home or at your local arts and crafts or DIY store. You will also need to find your nearest health or fragrance store to purchase essential oils; otherwise, you can always find a reputable company online to buy this item. Below you will find a list of tools and equipment you will need to start making candles at home.

Containers

The candle-making journey cannot come to its conclusion until the wax is poured into its mold. You can also buy a specific mold to pour your wax into, or you can use any household container that will be able to handle the heat of the job. These molds could include eggshells, mason jars, metal tins, or even old clay garden pots or mugs. You can essentially use any container as a mold as long as it is heat and fireproof.

Additionally, your mold size will depend on how much wax you will be melting down and the look you desire for your finished product. Moreover, you can even use cardboard boxes coated with vegetable oil to create your molds at home in various sizes to suit your needs. Wax is a highly flammable material; therefore, it is crucial to ensure that what you melt and pour your wax into is heat resistant.

Rubber gloves

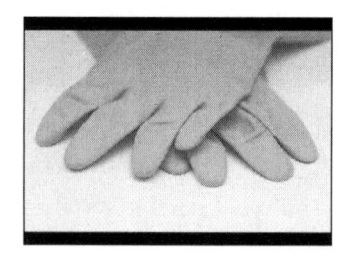

Be sure that before you begin your candle-making journey, you have safety gloves, either long protective rubber gloves for your hands or wear long sleeves to match the short gloves. Wearing safety gloves will ensure that any hot wax or potent oils won't come into contact with the skin on your hands, and you won't burn your arms. Similarly, you will need to ensure that your gloves are chemically resistant to the potent fragrance or essential oils and therefore won't come into contact with your skin.

Protective mask

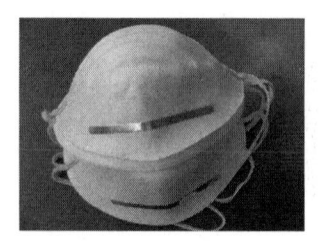

When working with candles, especially ones made from paraffin, it is vital to ensure that your workspace is thoroughly ventilated. This is to inhibit the inhalation of any chemical fumes produced during the melting of wax and adding of potent essential or fragrance oils during the candle-making process. By wearing an organic vapor respirator throughout your candle-making journey, you will substantially reduce the intake of harmful chemicals into your body.

Safety glasses

Protecting your eyes is crucial when you are candle-making, more so than your skin, but still of equal importance. Hot wax can cause irreparable damage to your eyes, especially if you are not wearing any protection. Therefore, it is imperative for you to wear a pair of safety glasses to prevent any backsplashes from reaching your eyes. Likewise, you will also need to make sure that your safety goggles are chemically resistant to avoid the absorption of the potent chemicals into the mucous membranes of your eyes.

Double boiler

For this method, a glass measuring cup will work best, and it is advised that this type of glass container may not handle repeated temperature fluctuations. This method is as low risk as heating for candle wax can get when it comes to candle making. However, the only downside is that it takes a longer time for the wax to melt; the benefit of this, though, is that it guarantees that your wax doesn't get burned.

Spatulas or spoons for mixing

You will need this item to stir your wax for even melting, mixing in colors or fragrances, as well as separating any larger chunks of wax. Similarly, you will also use the spatula or spoon to remove any leftover wax from the container in which you have melted your wax.

Measuring spoons

To ensure the success of your recipes, it is of utmost importance for you to be measuring out your ingredients to the exact weight required. By doing this, you can precisely measure all necessary ingredients before you begin making your candles.

Glass measuring cup

You will use this to melt your wax as well as stir in any fragrance or dyes that you have chosen. These measuring cups can be purchased in varying sizes and can be as large as 1000ml/27oz. All the while, they are super easy to clean.

Clothespins

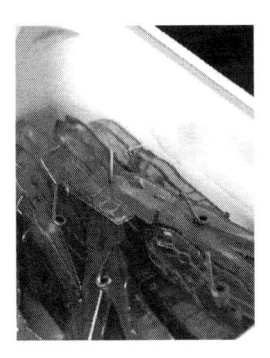

The best item to use as a beginner candle maker when it comes to setting your wick is a clothespin as they are cost-effective and reliable. Additionally, you can maneuver them easily for multi-wick applications or wide-diameter jars or containers. However, it is essential to note that you will need to have patience when centering your wick when it comes to clothespins. Alternatively, you can also purchase a wick bar if you are especially concerned about placing your wick in the dead center.

Kitchen scale

This item is vital for candle making as you will need to measure out everything like essential oils and wax. If you are serious about the craft, investing in an accurate kitchen scale will be worth the cost.

Glass thermometer

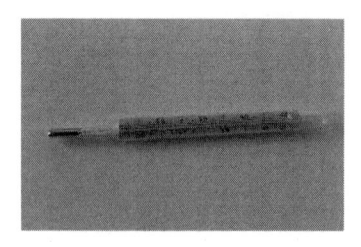

This tool will be essential for gauging the temperature of your wax accurately as it goes through the stages of heating and cooling. You will need to keep track of these different stages in the candle-making process as follows: Solid wax melts down into liquid wax. This Liquid wax + Essential/ fragrance oils = Solid wax + fragrance (finished candle).

To achieve the necessary temperatures required for each of these stages, you will have to have a glass thermometer at the very least. Otherwise, if you can afford to spend a bit more, you can get yourself an infrared heat gun. This tool uses unique infrared light waves that bounce off the surface of the wax to read the temperature.

This is done quickly and accurately without the need for a hands-on approach with no mess or fuss involved.

Wax additives (optional)

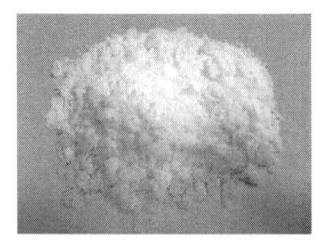

As the word suggests, these additives are artificial, and almost all candle-makers will choose a more natural alternative over artificial ones. Bear in mind, though, that candles will be generally fine without the need for these added extras, but there could be a time along your journey when you might be facing a specific problem that only an additive can solve.

Candle wax

Candle wax can be either natural or artificial in nature, and as you progress on your journey as a candle maker, it will be highly beneficial for you to know the difference between the two. Natural wax is biodegradable, sustainable, burns for a longer time than artificial waxes, and is easier to clean up. Regrettably, these natural waxes can be challenging to acquire even at your DIY or arts and crafts stores, so purchasing them online is going to be your best bet at acquiring these natural waxes.

Candle or wax dye (optional)

You can find candle dye in either liquid, flake, or solid form in an assortment of colors to suit your design needs. Each of these dyes is unique in its application and can be found at your local arts and crafts, DIY store, or online at retailers such as amazon. For starters, liquid dye is combined with melted wax and is blended evenly throughout your mixture. It provides a rich color to your finished candle.

Solid dye is made up of whole color segments (which are cut into small pieces), then mixed into your melted wax, and lastly, wax flakes are mixed in with melted wax for even distribution. These solid and flake dyes will give your finished candle more muted and pastel shades.

It is vital to take note that soy wax does not combine well with most dyes and will often produce a more muted shade. These dyes will come with their own manufacturer instructions, and it is up to you as the candle maker to follow these religiously.

Candle wicks

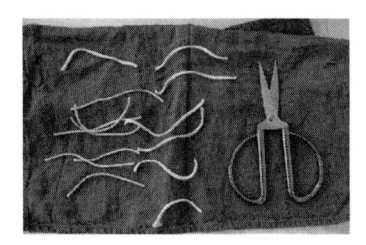

There are four basic kinds of candle wicks available on the market today and choosing the correct wick for your candle can be an intimidating process. Many variables will factor into choosing the proper wick type for your candle. These factors can include fragrance load, container diameter, type of wax dye, and the type of wax you will be using.

Candlewick tabs

These can be identified as tiny metal discs that can be fixed and secured to ensure the correct placement of the candle wick inside the candle. You can apply a small amount of heat-resistant glue, or you can use a small amount of melted wax to secure the wick to the bottom of the mold or container. Once attached, you can pour in your remaining wax, placing the wick in the center with a wick bar or clothespin to cool and solidify.

Essential oils (optional)

When it comes to scenting your candles, the possibilities are endless, and it is crucial to get your fragrance or essential oils from a reputable source that you trust. Unfortunately, there are many suppliers of low-quality, synthetic, or water down oils on the market, so you will need to do your research before committing to a brand and oil.

Mold sealer

Mold sealer is vital if you will be using a mold; otherwise, you will likely not need it. They can be acquired at your local arts, and crafts or DIY store or online and are used to block the hole you made in order to thread your wick through the base of the mold.

Tape measure

This tool will be indispensable as you will need it to measure the height and diameter of your container or mold for your candle wicks to sit at the appropriate height.

Drill

To make holes in your mold base, you will need either a drill or awl to get the job done. Having one of these two items on hand can make your candle molding process a whole lot simpler.

Fire extinguisher

As you will be working with wax, a flammable substance composed of mainly oil, you will need to invest in a dry chemical (ABC) type fire extinguisher to ensure that you are duly prepared if any fires break out. Most importantly, you should never forget to never throw water onto a wax fire as this can cause the wax to splash back and possibly burn you or others.

Chapter 4- Using Essential Oils

What are essential and fragrance oils?

Essential and fragrance oils are quite often confused with one another even though they are very different. The reality is that fragrances are artificial and are typically blended using synthetic products that have been watered down and diluted to have the same scent and quality needed as the original aroma it is trying to mimic. Essential oils, however, are purely obtained from natural plants and don't contain any synthetic chemicals or thinners.

The oils are acquired from either flowers, herbs, or roots, depending on the plant, and can even be extracted from leaves or seeds as well. Fragrances and essential oils can be a great additive to your candles, so don't be afraid to try new things.

Defining aromatherapy?

Aromatherapy can be described as the pseudoscience behind aromatic materials and other aroma-producing compounds like essential oils to achieve a heightened sense of emotional, spiritual, and physical well-being. Medicinally for aromatherapy to be considered genuine, the essential oils need to be 100% natural to be effective therapeutically.

Blending your own oils

To begin blending your own oils, you will first need to understand the basics of essential and fragrance oils. You will need to familiarise yourself with three scent notes, including head (top), heart (middle), and base notes, which help make up a well blended and harmonious oil. Here we will look at tools you will need, head, heart, and base notes, and how to combine them in the best ways possible to create the aroma you desire.

Tools

Paper and pen

Recording your results as you are working is a crucial step in the candle-making process. A pen and paper on hand will certainly benefit you when it comes to recording the quantities used to achieve your results. Skipping this step is not advised as it will be vital for checking on scents that you have previously made or that you want to create or tinker with in the future.

Gloves

When working with such potent oils, it is always advised to be wearing safety gloves to protect your skin. These natural oils are incredibly concentrated, and you wouldn't want the fragrance lingering on your skin while trying to make your own. It would only hinder the process with an unwanted scent.

Towels

As a candle maker, you will be all too familiar with the occasional spill; this is why it is essential to always have something absorbent on hand to deal with those out-of-the-blue spills. Now, as with all cautionary tales, accidents can happen, and it is in your best interest to be prepared when they do.

Small Glass Dropper or Blending Bottles

A small or large dropper or blending bottle will be essential for adding in essential oils with a no-mess, no-fuss approach. However, this will all be determined by the number of oils you will be blending. Therefore, you can find them in 0.04oz/1.1g, 0.12oz/3.5g, or 0.25oz/7.08g sizes when you are looking to purchase glass droppers.

Reducer caps or droppers

If you chose to use a blending bottle, these would typically come with their own reducer caps to control the flow of oils out of the bottle and into your blend. Similarly, if you purchase a glass dropper, it will also come with a pre-attached dropper to control the number of oils you will use. However, you will always need spares or extras depending on the number of essential oils you will be blending at once. You can achieve a similar result with an eyedropper or pipette if you don't have the other items available.

Perfume blotters, paper or cotton balls

Essential oils, like any other product, will have generic or knock-off products available on the market. You can use either of these items to test how well your blend turns out as it evaporates in the air. Given time these fragrance notes will change, and you will be able to smell the different layers of your fragrance oil as it dissipates into the air.

Scent notes

Scent notes come in a wide range of aromas but will typically be classified into seven main categories. These scent notes can come in a vast array of smells and aromas and what is listed here is only a fraction of the possibilities you can create.

- **Camphor-** These aromas are strong and heavy on the nose.
- **Herbaceous-** These notes will be earthy and pungent.
- **Citrus-** These notes provide a clean and refreshing aroma.
- **Floral-** These scent notes will be sweet and flowery.
- **Minty-** This scent note will provide you with a fresh and cool aroma.
- **Spicy-** These scent notes will have a sharp and piquant aroma.
- **Woodsy-** These scent notes will be earthy and uplifting, like the smell of fresh-cut wood.

The key to a successful blend is balancing these scent categories to create the perfect unison of aroma that is just right for you.

Headnotes

Head notes of essential oil blends will be the first to grab your attention. These notes provide a fresh, light, and airy aroma that can evaporate within ten minutes. Listed below are some head fragrance oils you can use to experiment and create your unique blend of essential oils.

Citrus

- Mandarin orange
- Grapefruit
- Lemongrass
- Lime
- Orange

Floral

- Neroli
- Palmarosa
- Lavender
- Rose
- Jasmine

Herbaceous

- Fennel
- Basil
- Coriander
- Galbanum (green resin)
- Sage

Minty

- Peppermint
- Spearmint

Spicy

- Cardamom
- Cinnamon
- Nutmeg

Camphor

- Cajeput
- Eucalyptus
- Citronella

Heart (middle) scent notes

Heart scent notes will be the focal point of your oil blend as they are more deeply rooted within your oil blend. These heart notes are crucial when blending as they are the foundation on which your other oils will stand. For the head and base notes to be noticed appropriately, you will need these heart notes to bring out the other oils' unique benefits. Listed below are a few of the middle fragrance oils you can use to create your own unique aroma blend for your candles.

Citrus

- Eucalyptus lemon
- Bergamot
- Grapefruit
- Petitgrain
- Lime

Floral

- Chamomile
- Geranium
- Jasmine
- Lavender
- Palmarosa

Herbaceous
- Bay leaf
- Citronella
- Clary sage
- Coriander
- Dill

Woodsy
- Pine
- Cyprus
- Spruce

Camphor
- Tee tree
- Ginger
- Camphor
- Pine
- Cajeput

Base scent notes

Base notes provide your oil with a dominating aroma that is most present after the other notes have already evaporated. These scent notes are more robust and last longer than that of the head (top), and heart (middle) notes. Listed below are a few of the base fragrance oils you can utilize to create your unique oil blend.

Citrus
- Lemongrass
- Orange
- Lime

Floral
- Ylang-Ylang

- Jasmine
- Rose

Herbaceous

- Angelica
- Rosemary
- Ginger
- Marjoram
- Basil

Minty

- Peppermint
- Spearmint

Camphor

- Eucalyptus
- Frankincense
- Pine
- Tea tree

Woodsy

- Sandalwood
- Myrrh
- Cedarwood

Spicy

- Cinnamon
- Clove
- Nutmeg
- Black pepper

Blending your own essential oils in 4 easy steps

When starting out as a novice blender, it will be in your best interest to begin with small batch sizes to test your fragrance. However, as you become more confident as a blender, you will be able to create more complex and aromatic blends. Therefore it is advised that when blending, you should always use a dilution of 20% in order to create the perfect mix for you that is well-balanced and harmonious. As a beginner, you should not be discouraged, as below there are four easy steps you can use to achieve your perfect blend.

Steps

1. To begin the process of blending your own oils, you will first need to pick between 3-4 essential oils of your choice for each head (top), heart (middle), and base note. While there is no limit to the number of oils you can blend, it is recommended that beginners start with no more than four oils max.
2. In order to achieve a uniform aroma that isn't overpowering, it is essential to use an equal amount for each of your essential oils. Don't forget to be making notes of your amounts and the processes you have followed so that you can look back on them for future use.
3. Start with one drop (0.002oz/0.05g) of oil for each of your head, heart, and base notes in a glass bottle. Shake together and analyze the scent you have created; at this stage, you can tinker by carefully adding in a drop at a time until you have reached your desired aroma.
4. Once you have created a scent of your liking, it is crucial for you to label your creation and the recipe for easy use in the future. Similarly, remember to be tracking the scent as it changes throughout the day or as you wear or test them.

Substituting essential oils

Oil	Substitution
Peppermint	Spearmint
Chamomile	Lavender
Neroli	Ylang-Ylang or Jasmine
Tangerine	Sweet orange
Bergamot	Grapefruit
Jasmine	Ylang-Ylang
Lemon	Grapefruit
Cinnamon	Clove
Vanilla	Peru Balsam or Benzoin

Chapter 5- Coloring Candles

Candle dyes (optional)

Specifically created to color candle wax, these dyes are chemically synthetic and are made using an oily chemical substrate known as anilines. They come in three distinct types, liquid, dye blocks, and flakes, which are water-soluble, all the while still producing a pleasing color for your candle. Liquid dyes provide rich colors, while flake and block dyes will give you more pale and pastel colors.

It is crucial to note that some fragrances and essential oils can change the color of your finished candle, so be sure to check the ingredients, usage instructions, and caution or warning labels before you begin.

Types of wax you can use for natural dyes.

If you color your candles naturally, first, you need to use the correct type of wax. Natural waxes such as palm, soy, and beeswax are just about the only natural waxes that will hold the color of the natural plant dye, and each of these wax types has its own ability to preserve color. Your best wax choice for natural dyes is soy wax, as it can combine with most colors well. Remember that when you are coloring with natural dyes, it is a labor and time-intensive process that could take up to two days for you to achieve the right color, unlike with synthetic dyes, which only take minutes.

Naturally coloring your candles

Natural colorants

Extracted from plants or minerals, natural dyes or pigments are non-synthetic or manufactured, meaning they are derived from 100% natural sources. Below is a list of plant extract that you can use for a more natural approach to dying your candles. As a plant dye, the natural color is extracted from the flowers, leaves, roots, or even stems, and certain plants will give you a better color than others. The only downside to coloring your candles naturally is the time it will take you to seep the color from the plant material into your melted wax. This process can take anywhere from 6-48 hours for the color to completely absorb, and the boldness of your color will depend on the plant material you are using.

Coloring soy wax naturally

Beige

- **Madder root-** This plan can be chopped, sliced, or dried and will give your wax a pink beige color.
- **Chamomile-** The flowers of this plant can be steeped into your wax to provide a soft beige color. Similarly, you can also use quality chamomile tea to achieve the same or similar color to the flowers.
- **Vanilla pods-** Vanilla pods can be cut open and sliced into pieces before being added to your wax and will provide a light beige to light brown color. Remember to note that you cannot use vanilla essence to color candles, only vanilla pods.

Light brown

- **Green tea-** Providing your wax with a light brown-green color, you will first need to ensure that your tea is not mixed in with other ingredients such as other teas. This plant is best used with the tea slightly crushed in a mortar and pestle and then placed in a coffee filter or tea bag to steep.
- **Sage-** Giving your wax a green-brown color, sage is best used with the leaves and stems lightly crushed in a mortar and pestle before placing them into a muslin sachet.
- **Henna-** This plant will allow your wax to turn a brown-olive color once steeped in a coffee filter instead of a muslin sachet or tea bag.

Brown

- **Cinnamon-** Use as either ground powder in a coffee filter or as individual crushed sticks for a soft, brown color.
- **Cloves-** This plant can be crushed lightly using a mortar and pestle, or you can also use a rolling pin and a muslin sachet to achieve a warm brown color for your wax.

Red

- **Rosehips-** When choosing rosehips to color candles with, it is better to use the darker colored rosehips instead of the green ones. These dark rose hips will give your wax a slight red-brown color once they have been slightly crushed in the mortar and pestle.
- **Alkanet root-** This root can be utilized chopped, sliced, and powdered to give your wax a more reddish hue. Remember, you will first need to crush the blocks or slices with a mortar and pestle before placing them within a coffee filter or muslin sachet to extract the most color possible.

Yellow

- **Annatto seeds-** These seeds can be used whole or ground and will give your wax a bright yellow to yellow-orange color. However, if you are using whole seeds, it will be easier to extract the color once they have been slightly crushed first.
- **Lemon peel-** Lemon peels can be used as grated or finely chopped pieces and will produce a more dull and muted yellow color or your wax.
- **Saffron-** This particular plant works well for coloring soy wax and will give your wax a soft and bright yellow color. Keep in mind that this plant is more costly than most, and it is best to use it in controlled circumstances. Therefore it is advised that when using saffron, always measure out the correct amount of wax and saffron to guarantee a warmer color for your wax.

- **Turmeric-** This yellow spice can be used dried and ground in a coffee filter or freshly sliced to give your wax a bold yellow color.
- **Safflower-** This plant's petals can be steeped in your wax to give a bright yellow color.

Orange

- **Orange peel-** For this plant fruit, you will need to use either the peel (sliced) or the zest (grated) of the orange to give your wax an orange hue.
- **Carrots-** You can use grated or finely chopped carrots in a coffee filter to give your wax a bold orange color, brighter than when using orange peels or zest. Keep in mind that if you are thinking of using purple carrots, these will give you an entirely different color, so be sure to experiment first.
- **Paprika-** For a dark orange color, ground paprika works best when seeped into the wax. Similarly, you can also use paprika peppers sliced into small pieces to color your wax. However, this will not produce as vivid of a color as the powdered form.

Green

- **Wheatgrass-** Wheatgrass can be used chopped or pulsed in a food processor or stick blender to achieve a bright green color. Be careful, however, not to juice the wheatgrass as this will not work to dye your wax.
- **Spirulina-** Providing your wax with a bold green color, spirulina powder is best used in a coffee filter because it is such a fine powder.
- **Rosemary-** Giving your wax a dull green color, rosemary is best used with the leaves stripped off the stem and then slightly crushed in a mortar and pestle.
- **Kelp-** This seaweed will provide your wax with a lovely green color similar to that of spirulina.

- **Nettle-** If you are looking for a more muted olive green, nettles are just the thing to look for. You can cut them into half-inch segments before steeping them using a muslin sachet.
- **Parsley-** There are many different types of parsley, and as such, you can experiment to find the best green for you. Simply lightly bruise the parsley before steeping.

Blue

- **Indigo-** A popular dye in the fashion industry, indigo is perfect for dying your wax a bright and bold blue.

Preparing your plant material for dying

Steps

1. Gather the plant material that you are going to be using, like the roots, stems, leaves, and flowers or a combination of each.
2. Cut your plant material into small pieces as this will aid in the extraction of the color from the plants. If you are working with wheatgrass, you can stick it in the food processor or use a stick blender for a few short bursts to achieve a rough chop. Be careful, however, not to over blend the wheatgrass as you don't want to juice it.
3. Now put the pieces of plant material into either a heatproof bag, muslin sachet, coffee filter, or heat resistant tea bag. If you are using the muslin sachet or coffee filter, bear in mind that you will need to secure the end with either cooking twine or a piece of the wick to keep your material inside.
4. Next, you can begin to slowly lower your sachet into your meted wax until it is completely submerged but not enough that it touches the bottom of your boiler. Remember to note that while your plant matter is seeping, the temperature of your wax should not exceed between 130-140F/54-60C.

5. Wait for your plants to seep their color into the wax, be patient as this process can take anywhere from 6 hours to two days, depending on the plant material you have used. Some of the colors may remain quite pastel, and after 24-48 hours, the color is unlikely to get any darker or more profound.
6. Once you have obtained the color you desire, you can now remove the sachet of plant material from your wax, being careful not to burn yourself with the hot wax in the process. If some plant material happens to make its way into your wax, you will need to strain it out before pouring your wax into its mold because you don't want dead plant material to rot inside your candle.
7. Give your wax one more stir before you put the wax into your pre-wicked mold to guarantee that the color is distributed evenly throughout the wax.

How to test your candle dye color

Steps

1. Cut strips of white paper into 5-inch/12.7cm strips to conduct your color tests.

2. Next, dip your strip of white paper into your colored wax, remove and watch it solidify. This is going to be the color of your finished candle once it has been set.

3. If you are not happy with the color or shade you have, you can make any adjustments now. To achieve a more profound and bolder color, you will need to add more dye to your mix. For a more pastel shade, you can add in some white. (You can skip this step if you are satisfied with your color test)

4. If you will be adding fragrance or essential oils into your wax blend, it is vital to do the strip test before you begin adding them in. This step is essential if you do not want to

burn away any aroma or risk losing any of your candle's scents.

What not to color your candles with.

There are many ways in which you can color your candles, but there are also ways in which you shouldn't. These dyes listed below are in no way a good substitute for the real thing and should be avoided when coloring your candles, as they can cause adverse effects or possibly ruin your batch entirely.

Mica Powder- A popular natural mineral ingredient in cosmetic products such as lipsticks, lip balms, soaps, and bath bombs for its bright and bold colors and skin-safe attributes. However, as beautiful as the color may turn out to be in your finished candle, they, unfortunately, won't burn well or even light at all. Fortunately, mica powders can be used relatively well in wax melts as there is no need for a wick.

Food coloring- Although you can use this to dye a multitude of food-related items, as the name suggests, food coloring is not a good option when it comes to coloring candles. This is because food coloring does not bond well with candles because of certain ingredients usually present, such as corn syrup, alcohol, glycerin, water, citric acid, or propylene glycol. These compounds cannot bond with candle wax and therefore sink to the bottom, or pool in beads on top of the wax, making food coloring an unwise choice for coloring your candles.

Crayons- Widely popular nowadays because of DIY and arts and craft Youtubers, however contrary to their belief, crayons aren't actually meant to color candle wax. Why may you ask? Crayons are made of mainly paraffin wax, and candles are wax, so in theory, it should work, right? Wrong.

The "most" part is the problem when it comes to crayons, as they also contain other compounds such as powdered colorants like pigments and oxides. But, as eye-catching and bold as they may be, the candle won't burn for long or before it even has a chance to pool around the wick.

Pigments and oxides- These types of powdered pigments are popular in items such as crayons, beauty products, and arts and crafts tools, to name a few. As these pigments or oxides are typically oil dispersible and soluble, these powdered pigments will have the same problem as crayons of not burning for that long or at all.

Chapter 6- The Fundamentals of Candle Making

Candle Making wax temperatures

- Bayberry Candles- 180-210F/82.2-98.8C
- Dipping candles- 160-165F/71.1-73.8C
- Container candles- 130F/54.4C
- Taper candles- 158F/70C

Wax temperatures for candle molds

- Glass molds- 170-200F/76.6-93C
- Acrylic molds- 180-210F/82.2-99C
- Metal molds- 180-210F/82.2-99C
- Rubber molds- 160-180F71.1-82C
- Tear away molds (such as corrugated cardboard)- 160F/71C

Curing your candles

The process of candle curing can be defined as wax becoming resistant to heat by hardening at a molecular level to enable scent molecules to be evenly distributed throughout the set candle. Therefore, this means that depending on the type of wax you are using will vary the curing time of your candle, so be sure to check your wax before you begin. Below is a list of five average curing times, along with their wax types.

Wax type	Average cure time
Paraffin	3-5 days
beeswax	10 days
Parra Soy (Paraffin and soy blend)	7-10 days
Palm	5-7 days
Soy	14 days

Conducting a simple burn test

In order to see if your candle passes a burn test, it will need to be put through a process of testing to ensure your candle is safe and meets performance requirements. These tests can take weeks at a time to be completed correctly, depending on the size of your candle. The main focus of a candle burn test is to check the relationship between your wax and wick and how well the scent dissipates as your candle is burning once it has been set. Specifically speaking, a burn test will allow you to see if you are using the correct wick for your candle or if you will need to make adjustments.

What you will need to do before conducting your test

Before you begin conducting your burn test, you will need to ensure that a few measures are in place first.

1. Firstly, your candles should be about 8 inches away from each other, with clearly marked times and dates displayed.

2. Secondly, the temperature of your room should be no more than 68-86F/20-30C to provide consistency for your results.

3. Lastly, you should have a large enough tray beneath your candles to catch the entire melt pool as the candle burns.

The primary burn test procedure

While following industry safety standards is not a requirement, you should be voluntarily adhering to them as standard practice as a candle maker. This means that although you don't have to follow each and every standard, you need to follow the basics for providing a safe burning candle. To do this, you will need to burn your candles consistently and consecutively over a few days or weeks, considering that different candle types will burn differently. For instance, gel candles will need to burn for eight-hour periods, tea light candles for a single burn until they have melted down, and any other candles will need four-hour increments. In addition, a standard burn test will need to be conducted as follows:

<u>Steps</u>

1. Prepare to burn your candles by following the pre-burn instructions.
2. Trim your wick to ¼ of an inch/0.6cm for every candle you will be testing.
3. Once you have lit your candle and after the candle has burned, you will need to record your findings. Additionally, for every hour after, you will need to record and visually observe if there are any changes like the ones below:
    - Your container is not cracked or broken.
    - Your flame's maximum height is less than three inches/7.6cm for regular candles or three and ¾ of an inch/9.5cm for religious purposes.
    - No black smoke is excessively coming from the wick.
    - Your container has damaged the surface it has been on.
    - Your candle hasn't fallen over or spilled its contents.
4. Record the height of your candle flame at four-hour increments, even if you are observing it every hour.

5. If the candle has failed to meet any of the requirements mentioned in step three, then the candle can be marked as a failed test.
6. Once your candle cools, you will need to repeat steps three to six until your candle is fully melted down or has failed the test.

Conducting a basic melt pool test

Steps

1. To begin, start by trimming your candle wick to ¼ of an inch/0.6cm. If you are conducting more than one test, it is crucial to label each candle for reference.
2. Next, place your candles onto a flat, clean and heat-resistant surface, keeping each candle three-six inches/7.6-15.2cm apart. You should have a clean line of vision to the candles as you will need to monitor them as they burn. It is not recommended to leave any candle burning unattended.
3. Now you can light your candle or candles (if you are doing a significant test), and remember to note the time you lit each one. Never leave a candle burning without supervision.
4. Once two hours have passed, you can make a note of the melt pool and the appearance of your wick. Typically, the melt pool should achieve the desired diameter at this stage, but if not, it is most likely because your wick is too small.
5. When four hours have lapsed, you will need to re-record your results before softly blowing the flame out. By this stage, your melt pool should be about ½ an inch/1.2cm deep. However, if your candle wick is shooting, mushrooming, or if the melt pool is subsequently deeper than ½ an inch/.2cm, then the wick is probably too big.
6. Lastly, allow your candle to cool for a minimum of five hours before repeating steps three to five until your candle has completely burned down. Keep in mind that the caliber of the burn will almost certainly change while you are burning the entire candle.

Test results

Wick was the incorrect size or was too hot if:

- Carbon balls larger than 3/16 of an inch or 0.5cm have formed.
- The height of the flame is more significant than three inches/7.6cm or three and ¾ /9.5cm, if for religious use.
- The temperature of your container exceeds 140F/60C
- The melt pool is too large.

Your candle needs multiple wicks, or the wick was too small if:

- Your flame keeps dying before the candle has a chance to burn.
- There are large amounts of wax present around the edges even after multiple burns.
- There is a large amount of wax on the sides in addition to the candle tunneling.

Candle making methods

Making a simple molded candle

Steps

1. Gather the tools and equipment necessary in addition to preparing your workstation surface by lining it with wax paper for easy cleanup.
2. Prepare the amount of wax you will need to fill your mold. You can easily do this by first measuring your mold using water, keeping in mind that 3.5lbs/1.6kgs of water will equal 3lbs/1.4kgs of wax. Once you have measured your mold, be sure to dry it out thoroughly before using it.
3. Now you can begin breaking your wax-up into smaller, more manageable pieces by either cutting it into small cubes of about one inch/2.5cm or shaving it into flakes with a knife. Alternatively, you can also place the wax slab into a sealable

plastic bag (i.e., garbage bag), and using a hammer; you can smash the wax into smaller chunks.
4. Next, you can place your wax chunks/flakes into your double boiler to begin melting.
5. Keeping an eye on your wax as it melts, checking to ensure that your wax gets to the correct temperature. You can do this accurately using your thermometer, being careful, however, not to let the bottom of your thermometer come into contact with the base of your boiler bowl.
6. Now you can start reducing the heat of your double boiler to between medium and low in order to keep the water at a simmering boil. Be careful not to let your water dry up as it is boiling, as this could spoil your wax.
7. In the next step, as you are waiting for your wax to melt, you can begin by lightly coating the inside of your mold (if you are using a mold) with mold release. You can forget this step if you are using a container mold.
8. Once you have coated your mold, you can then begin to cut your wick to the correct length for your recipe or as desired.
9. Next, you can start by threading your wick through your candle mold, covering it thoroughly using a mold sealer which will stick the wick to the outside of your mold, preventing any leaks.
10. Once your wick has been secured to the exterior of your mold, you can begin straightening it through the center. Remember to pull the wick taught before wrapping it around your clothes peg or skewer. Similarly, remember to ensure that the clothes peg or skewer sits flush against the surface of your mold and is well centered.
11. Your wax should be melted at this stage and checked to ensure the correct temperature has been met. Once you have the proper temperature, you can now add in any additives (if any errors have occurred); otherwise, you can skip this step.
12. You can add in your dyes in his next step, making sure to stir until thoroughly and evenly combined into your mixture.

13. Next, you can add your fragrance or essential oils or your own blend just before you are ready to pour your wax into its mold. Keep in mind that you can lose aroma if you add your oils to your wax when it is too hot.
14. Now that you have added in all your extras like color and scent, you can begin to slowly pour your melted wax into its mold until it is about 90% full. Next, gently tap the base of your mold to remove any leftover air pockets in your mixture, and any leftover wax can be poured into a tin and set aside.
15. Allow your wax to cool, keeping in mind that a small indent will form around the wick as it cools. However, you can quickly fix this by remelting your leftover wax and slowly filling in the cavity, being careful not to overfill. Leave aside to cool once again.
16. Now that your candle is cool, you can start by gently removing the clothes peg or skewer from the top of the mold. You can now tip the candle upside down, and it should slide freely from the mold, thanks to the mold sealer.
17. Lastly, you can trim the bottom end of your wick so that it is flush with the base of your candle. Additionally, you will also shorten the top of your candle wick to about ¼ of an inch/0.6cm high or as you desire.

Making a basic container candle

<u>Steps</u>

1. First, you will need to gather all the tools and equipment necessary and prepare your workstation by laying out wax paper onto the surface.
2. Next, you will need to preheat your oven to 150-170F/65-76C or the lowest setting available for your containers. Now place your containers onto a baking tray and put them in the oven. This will prevent any cracks or breaks from forming as well as avoid any possible jump lines.

3. Weigh out the amount of wax you will be using to fill your containers, considering that 3.5lbs/1.6kgs of water is equal to 3lbs/1.4kgs of wax.
4. Next, you will need to heat your wax in your double boiler at a temperature of 170-180F/76-82C or medium heat, as the water does not need to be at a rolling boil. Additionally, you must always keep checking the temperature of your wax as you do not want it to get too hot.
5. In this next step, you will need to measure out and add in your fragrance or essential oils once your wax is at the correct temperature. However, the standard practice for fragrance or essential oils is 1oz/28.3g of scent per 1lb/454g of wax.
6. Now you can measure and add your dye to your wax mixture, mixing until thoroughly combined. It is advised not to overdo the amount of color you put in, as you cannot remove it once it has been added.
7. Test your color using your white paper strips. If you are unsatisfied, you can always add in more dye.
8. You can begin to mix your ingredients together for about 2-3 minutes, making sure that they are incorporated evenly throughout your mixture. If there is still oily residue on the surface of your wax, you will need to continue mixing until it has thoroughly combined with your wax.
9. Next, you will need to set your wick onto the bottom of your container using either heat-resistant glue or wick stickers.
10. Once your wick is centered, you can now begin to pour in your melted wax until it fills the widest part of your container. Do not pour your wax too fast as this will cause backsplashes that could get onto your skin or clothes, and leave dried wax on the inside of your container. Similarly, you can also cause air pockets to appear on the surface of your wax if you rush to pour it quickly into the container.
11. In this next step, you will need to secure your wick using either a wick bar, metal skewer, or clothes peg. You can do this by pulling your wick taught gently before either slotting

it into the wick bar, wrapping it around the metal skewer, or clothespin before placing it onto the rim of the container. Now you can set aside your containers to cool, being careful not to bump or move them unnecessarily.

12. Now that your candle has completely cooled, you can remove the wick holder. You will notice that a small indent has appeared around the exposed section of your wick. This is an easy fix and can be resolved by simply pouring a bit more melted wax into the cavity to fill and even it out.
13. Now you can trim the top of your wick to ¼ of an inch/0.6cm long or as desired for decorative purposes. Be careful, however, not to cut your wick too short as this will prevent the candle from burning properly. If desired, you can also fit the lid of the container back onto the jar.
14. Lastly, as an extra precaution, you can add a warning or caution label to the base of your container, which will be personal to you or to your business.

Making a basic votive candle

Steps

1. Begin by blending in 25% beeswax to 75% soy wax, as this particular blend will give your candle a longer burn and a more pungent scent.
2. Next, you will need to create your double boils by filling a saucepan with water and heating it on medium-high heat. Now you can place your glass measuring jug, bowl, or pouring pot with your wax pieces onto the rim of the saucepan. Remember to make sure the bottom of your bowel doesn't meet the base of your double boiler, then heat your wax to the required temperature.
3. Once your wax has begun melting, you can now start by adding in your dye as desired for the color you are looking for. You can test the color of your set candle before you pour them by doing a strip test with a piece of white paper. If you

are unsatisfied with your color, keep adding in small amounts until you are happy with the color produced,

4. Now that your dye has been added, be sure to keep monitoring the temperature of your wax. It will need to be heated to 170F/76C, stirring gently but continuously, taking measures to not let your wax get too high of a temperature, typically 200F/93C. When making votive candles, it is crucial to never let the wax get to temperatures above 170-180F/76-82C, as anything hotter will burn your wax.

5. In this next step, while you are waiting for your wax to come to temperature, start preparing your molds by coating them with a mold releaser before inserting the pins inside the mold.

6. When your molds are ready, you can begin adding in your aroma, but only once your wax has reached 145F/63C. Do not add in your cent into your wax when it is too hot, as this will cause the aromas to burn off and the scent to weaken. Keep stirring gently until your scent is thoroughly combined.

7. With your scent now incorporated and your wax cooled to 125-130F/52-54C, you can directly pour your wax. To do this, start by slowly pouring your wax into your votive molds, filling them to the top being sure not to overfill them. Before pouring into your other mold, be sure to mix your wax to ensure even scent distribution throughout your batch. Keep any extra wax to fill any gaps or air pockets in your mixture while it is cooling. This will take about 10 minutes. Now that your candle has cooled, you can begin to re-heat your leftover wax until it just melted to fill the cavities that may have appeared around the base of your wick until they are level.

8. Before you try to release your votive candle from the mold, they will first need to cure for eight hours to guarantee easy release from the mold. To remove the candle, you should turn it upside down, and the candle should easily slip from the mold by lightly tapping the base.

9. To wick your now cooled candles, you must first pull out the pins threading the wick through the currently vacant holes. Next, secure the wick by gently pushing on the metal disc at the wick base to prevent it from dislodging from the candle. When wicking your candles as a beginner, using pre-tabbed wicks will be the most straightforward option for you. You can trim your wick to ⅛ of an inch/ or as desired. Your candle is now ready to light.

Tea light candles made easy

Steps

1. First, gather all the equipment and tools you will need and start by weighing out your wax using a kitchen scale. Next, start melting your wax in a double boiler until your wax is at 185F/85C.
2. As you are waiting for your wax to melt, you can start preparing your tea light cups. Place a wick sticker to the base of your pre-tabbed wicks before centering them and sticking them down onto the tea light cups.
3. Once your wax has reached 185F/85C, you can add in your dye, stirring gently until it is evenly distributed throughout your mixture.
4. Next, you can add your fragrance or essential oils once you have removed your wax from the heat. You can then begin mixing it for about two minutes until the scent is well incorporated with your wax, then set aside to cool.
5. Now that your wax has cooled to 135F/57C, you can begin pouring your wax into your tea light cups slowly, being careful not to overpour the wax.
6. With your wax now poured, you can begin to center your wick in each tea light candle to guarantee a safe burn.
7. Lastly, you will need to leave your candles overnight to cure before you can use them.

Making a floating candle from scratch

<u>Steps</u>

1. Begin by first gathering all the tools and equipment you will need, such as essential oils, dyes, and wicks, etc.
2. Following this, you can add your wax into your double boiler once your water has pre-boiled. You can then heat your wax to 185F/85C.
3. While your wax is melting, you can now add in your wax dye to ensure even color distribution throughout.
4. Next, you will need to maintain a constant temperature of 150F/65C for your paraffin wax to be ready for pouring. To guarantee you have the correct temperature, it is advised to use a thermometer to check the way throughout the heating process.
5. As you wait for your wax to come to temperature, you can start coating the inside of your baking tray with a mold release as you will be removing them from the tray by the delicate wick of the candle. If you do not precoat your molds beforehand, you will have difficulty removing them from the tray.
6. Now that your molds are ready, you can begin adding in your dye, taking measures to ensure that your color is well mixed in before moving onto the next step.
7. Now that your wax is ready to pour, you can turn off the heat before adding in your scents to eliminate the possibility of any aroma being burnt away. Once your blend has been added, you can slowly pour your wax into the tray as evenly as possible.
8. Once your wax is poured, wait for a few minutes before you start adding in your wicks. They should be standing on their own once centered; otherwise, using a toothpick, you can fix them if necessary.
9. With your wicks now centered and secure, give your candles time to cure and solidify. You will need to wait for two hours

after the wicks have set before attempting to remove them from the tray.
10. Lastly, once you have ensured your candles are set by giving them enough time to cure, you can gently pull them up and out by the tray, using the tips of the wick. You can wipe away any excess material before leaving them aside to set completely. Once fully cured, you can place them into any body of water.

Making a floating candle from a tea light candle

Steps

1. First, gather your tea light candles and begin removing them from their cups by turning them upside down.
2. Next, using a lit taper candle (as these are the easiest to work with), drip a small amount of wax from the taper candle onto the bottom of the tea light candle until the wick holder is sealed entirely with wax.
3. Your candles are now ready to float in any body of water you may choose. However, keep in mind that these candles don't burn for longer than 30-45 minutes when in water.

Pillar candles made easy

Steps

1. Gather all the tools and equipment necessary to begin.
2. Cut and measure out your wax using a kitchen scale and a glass measuring jug.
3. The wax will now need to be melted at a temperature of 180F/82C using your double boiler. However, the double boiler temperature will need to be lowered to a medium-low to keep the water from splashing out the boiler. You will need to keep checking the temperature of your wax to ensure it doesn't burn.
4. As you are waiting for your wax to melt, you can prepare the molds by cleaning them out first and then adding the wicks, which you will need to cut to length. Thread the wicks

through the hole in the base of your mold, leaving a few inches free before holding it securely to the base and using the mold sealer, press the wick and the sealer firmly to the bottom, ensuring no gaps for leaks.

5. Next, you must anchor your wick to the top of your mold using either a metal skewer, wick bar, or clothes peg, pulled tightly to center it evenly.

6. Now you can measure your dye and add it to your wax mixture. You can do a strip test with a piece of white paper to check the final color of your candle. If you are not happy with the color, you can continue adding in small amounts of dye until you reach the desired color.

7. Once your molds are prepared and you have added in your color, you can now add your fragrance or essential oils into your melted wax, stirring until fully incorporated evenly.

8. Next, you will need to stir all your ingredients together thoroughly before pouring your wax into its mold. It is recommended that the wax is between 185-200F/85-93 C before being poured level with the top of the mold. Do not pour your wax too quickly, as this can cause air pockets to form on the surface of your wax. Any leftover wax can be kept aside to be remelted for the second pour.

9. Now you will need to poke some relief holes into your candle to aid in the release of any air pockets that may have formed as the wax shrinks and cools. You can poke our relief holes once a skin has formed on your wax; one for each side of your wick should be sufficient. Ensure that the holes are deep enough; however, do not puncture the sides of the mold in the process but make sure that the holes are large enough to form a tunnel for your second pour. You will need to do this a few times while your wax is cooling, and you won't be able to pour the wax a second time until your wax is completely set.

10. With your candle now cool, you can use your leftover wax heated to 180F/82C to fill in any cavities that you created within the first hour. You will need to ensure that your

second pour is even with your first one, although you will end up with a "seam" line on your finished candle.
11. You can remove your candle from its mold by first taking out the screw as well as the mold putty from the bottom of the mold. Now you should gently slide the mold from the candle; however, if it doesn't come off quickly, you can put it into the freezer for 5 minutes to aid in the release from the mold. If unsuccessful, repeat, but do not leave your candle in for too long. This can cause cracks to form, resulting in your candle falling apart when you remove it from the mold. Additionally, you can use the wick to help remove your candle, pulling gently as too much force can result in the wick breaking or coming out of your candle.
12. Lastly, you can finish off your candle by trimming the top wick to ¼ of an inch/0.6cm in length, taking caution not to cut the wick too short.

How to make a simple gel candle

Steps

1. First, gather all the tools and equipment you will need as well and prepare your workstation for use.
2. Prepare your glass container with a small amount of heat-resistant glue and stick down your wick, taking care to center it before leaving it to dry too quickly.
3. Next, start cutting your gel wax into more manageable pieces before placing them into your double boils to melt at medium heat.
4. Keeping an eye on your temperature is crucial as you will need to keep the temperature of your gel wax at 200F/93C. This is the ideal heat for your gel wax to turn smooth, transparent, and translucent.
5. Now you can begin to slowly add in your dye until you have achieved the color you desire. If you will be embedding items into your wax, it is better to use less dye to make out the objects within.

6. In this next step, you can begin adding your fragrance or essential oils taking care to mix them in thoroughly.
7. Preheat your containers to about 150-160F/66-71C in a microwave or oven to eliminate air pockets showing up inside your gel wax.
8. If you will be embedding any items into your gel wax, now is the time to do so. Placement for visibility is essential so set the imbeds near to the edges of your container (if not, skip this step).
9. Next, you can set your container on a flat surface with the side tilted. You can slowly pour in your hot wax down the inside of your container. This step should help eliminate any chance of bubbles forming inside of your gel.
10. Following pouring, you can now straighten out your wick, twisting the end around a skewer or clothes peg to keep the wick centered and straight.
11. Finally, you can set your candle aside to cool completely before trimming the wick of ¼ of an inch/0.6cm long. Be careful not to snip the wick too close to the wax as the candle will have difficulty burning.

Chapter 7- 35 Simple Candle Recipes

1. Simple relaxation candle recipe

- 3oz/85g of Soy wax
- 1.5oz/30g of Jojoba/Avocado/Almond oil
- 0.2oz/5.7g of Vitamin E oil
- 30 drops of Essential or fragrance oils of your choice
- Wicks
- Glass container or tin

Method: Follow the instructions for making a basic container candle.

2. Easy massage candle

- 2.8oz/80g of Soy wax
- 0.9oz/25g of Shea or cocoa butter; otherwise, you can use a combination of both.
- 0.5oz/14.2g of Coconut oil

- 0.5oz/14.2g of Jojoba/Avocado or Almond oil
- 0.05oz/ of Vitamin E oil
- 12 drops of lavender essential oil
- 12 drops of rose absolute
- 20 drops of grapefruit essential oil
- 2 drops of Ylang-ylang
- 10 drops of coriander essential oil
- Glass containers
- Candle wicks

Method: Follow the instructions for making a basic container candle.

3. Basic Beeswax candle

- 12oz/340g of Beeswax
- 12oz/340g Organic palm oil or shortening
- Glass containers
- Square braided cotton wick

Method: Follow the instructions for making a basic container candle.

4. Coffee and vanilla-scented candles

- 4oz/113.4g of Soy wax chips

- Whole coffee beans
- Whole vanilla beans, chopped
- 100drops of essential coffee oil
- 100 drops of vanilla essential oil
- Glass containers
- Candlewick

Method: Follow the instructions for making a basic container candle.

5. Lemon and rosemary-scented candles

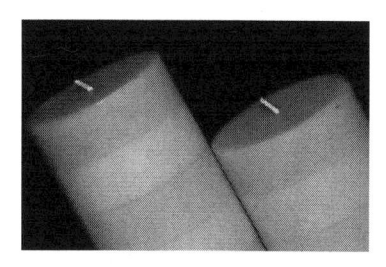

- 1lb/454g of Paraffin wax
- Candle wicks
- Glass containers
- 40 drops of Rosemary essential oil
- 40 drops of Lemon essential oil

Method: Follow the instructions for making a basic container candle.

6. Lavender essence scented candle

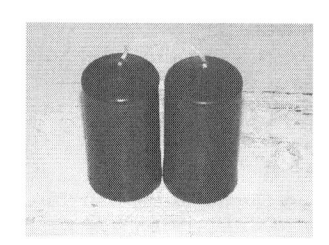

- 1lb/454g of soy Wax
- Red wax dye

- 5-10 drops of Lavender essential oil
- Glass containers
- Candle wicks

Method: Follow the instructions for making a basic container candle.

7. Honeysuckle oil candle

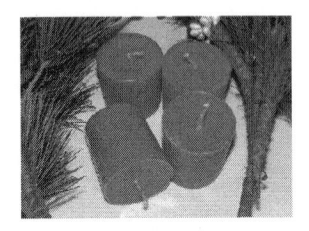

- 1lb/454g of soy Wax
- Red dye
- 5-10 drops of Honeysuckle oil
- Glass containers
- Candle wicks

Method: Follow the instructions for making a basic container candle.

8. Soothing Sandalwood and Jasmine Candle

- 1lb/454g of soy wax
- Brown wax dye
- 5-10 drops of Sandalwood essential oil
- 5-10 drops of Jasmine essential oil
- Glass container
- Candle wicks

Method: Follow the instructions for making a basic container candle.

9. Tropical Coconut scented candles

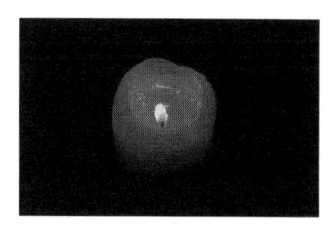

- 1lb/454g of soy wax
- Red wax dye
- 5-10 drops of Coconut essential oil
- Glass containers
- Candle wicks

Method: Follow the instructions for making a basic container candle.

10. Spicy Ginger scented candles

- 1lb/454g of soy wax
- Brown wax dye
- 5-10 drops of Ginger essential oil
- Glass containers
- Candle wicks

Method: Follow the instructions for making a basic container candle.

11. Earthy scented candles

- 1lb/454g of soy wax
- Green wax dye
- 5-10 drops of Pine essential oil
- 5-10 drops of Cedarwood essential oil
- Glass containers
- Candle wicks

Method: Follow the instructions for making a basic container candle.

12. Absolute honey candles

- 1lb/454g of soy wax
- Yellow wax dye
- 5-10 drops of Honey absolute essential oil
- Glass containers

- Candle wicks

Method: Follow the instructions for making a basic container candle.

13. Rose scented candles

- 1lb/454g of soy wax
- Blue wax dye
- 5-10 drops of Rose essential oil
- Glass containers
- Candle wicks

Method: Follow the instructions for making a basic container candle.

14. Mango Butter essence

- 1lb/454g of soy wax
- Yellow wax dye
- 5-10 drops of Mango butter essential oil
- Glass containers
- Candle wicks

Method: Follow the instructions for making a basic container candle.

15. Spicy Clove essence

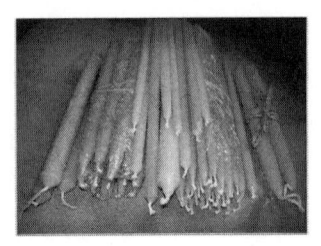

- 1lb/454g of soy wax
- Yellow wax dye
- 5-10 drops of Clove essential oil
- Glass containers
- Candle wicks

Method: Follow the instructions for making a basic container candle.

16. Tropical Paradise

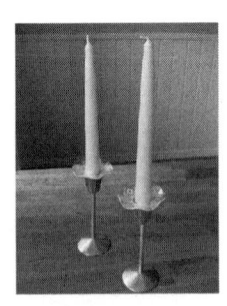

- 1lb/454g of soy wax
- Yellow wax dye
- 5-10 drops of Pineapple essential oil
- Glass containers
- Candle wicks

Method: Follow the instructions for making a basic container candle.

17. Pretty in Pink

- 1lb/454g of soy wax
- Pink wax dye
- 5-10 drops of Pomegranate essential oils
- Glass containers
- Candle wicks

Method: Follow the instructions for making a basic container candle.

18. An apple a day

- 1lb/454g of soy wax
- Green wax dye
- 5-10 drops of Apple essential oil
- Glass containers
- Candle wicks

Method: Follow the instructions for making a basic container candle.

19. This is Halloween

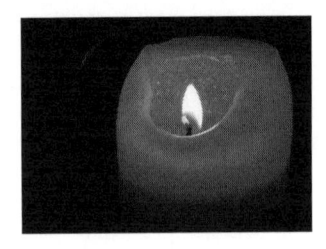

- 1lb/454g of soy wax
- Orange wax dye
- 5-10 drops of Pumpkin essential oil
- Glass containers
- Candle wicks

Method: Follow the instructions for making a basic container candle.

20. Festive Delight

- 1lb/454g of soy wax
- Red wax dye
- 2 drops of pine,
- 2 drops of clove
- 2 drops of Berries,
- 2 drops of Cinnamon
- 2 drops of Nutmeg.
- Glass containers
- Candle wicks

Method: Follow the instructions for making a basic container candle.

21. Cinnamon Essentials

- 1lb/454g of soy wax
- Brown wax dye
- 5-10 drops of Cinnamon essential oils
- Glass containers
- Candle wicks

Method: Follow the instructions for making a basic container candle.

22. Wine Lovers Dream

- 1lb/454g of soy wax
- Red wax dye
- 5-10 drops of Grapeseed or grape essential oil
- Glass containers
- Candle wicks

Method: Follow the instructions for making a basic container candle.

23. Mind, Body, and Relaxation

- 1lb/454g of soy wax
- 5-10 drops of Frankincense essential oil
- Glass containers
- Candle wicks

Method: Follow the instructions for making a basic container candle.

24. Natures Garden

- 1lb/454g of soy wax
- Pink wax dye
- A small sprinkling of dried herbs of your choice (i.e., Rosemary, Thyme, or Basil, etc.)
- Glass containers
- Candle wicks

Method: Follow the instructions for making a basic container candle.

25. Japanese Cherry Blossom Season

- 1lb/454g of soy wax
- Pink wax dye
- 5-10 drops of Cherry blossom essential oil
- Glass containers
- Candle wicks

Method: Follow the instructions for making a basic container candle.

26. Apple Pie Surprise

- 1lb/454g of soy wax
- Green wax dye
- 5-10 drops of Apple essential oil
- Powdered Cinnamon
- Glass containers
- Candle wicks

Method: Follow the instructions for making a basic container candle.

27. Strawberry Fever

- 1.5lbs/680.4g of soy wax
- Red wax dye
- 10-15 drops of strawberry essential oil
- Glass containers
- Candle wicks

Method: Follow the instructions for making a basic container candle.

28. Rosemary and Lavender

- 32oz/907.2g of Soy wax flakes
- 20-30 drops of lavender essential oil
- 20-30 drops of Rosemary essential oil
- 0.06oz/1.7g dried and ground rosemary and lavender flowers (per candle, optional)
- Glass containers
- Candle wicks

Method: Follow the instructions for making a basic container candle.

29. Tea Tree, Lavender, and Rosemary

- 1lb/454g of Soy wax/12oz/340.2g of soy + 4oz/113.4 of beeswax (blended)
- 6 drops of Rosemary essential oil
- 2 drops of Lavender essential oil
- 2 drops of Teatree essential oil
- Glass containers
- Candle wicks

Method: Follow the instructions for making a basic container candle.

30. Citronella Candles

- 1lb/454g of soy wax
- 5-10 drops of Citronella oil
- Glass containers
- Candle wicks

Method: Follow the instructions for making a basic container candle.

31. Zesty Lemon Candles

- 1lb/454g of Wax
- 1oz of Lemon essential oils
- Wax dye (optional)
- Glass containers
- Candle wicks

Method: Follow the instructions for making a basic container candle.

32. Simple Votive Candles

- 1lb/454g of Paraffin wax
- 0.17oz of Vybar 260
- 1oz/28.3g of your chosen essential oils
- Glass containers
- Candle wicks

Method: Follow the instructions for making a basic votive candle.

33. Simple Floating Candles

- 1lb/454g of melt point Paraffin wax
- 0.3oz/8.5g of Vybar 103
- 1oz/28.3g of your chosen essential oils
- Wax dye of your color choice (optional)
- Glass containers
- Candle wicks

Method: Follow the instructions for making a floating candle from scratch.

34. Easy Tea Light Candles

- 1lb of melt point paraffin wax
- 0.3oz/8.5g of Vybar 103
- 1oz/28.2g of your choice of essential oils
- Wax dye of your color choice (optional)
- Tea light cups
- Candle wicks

Method: Follow the instructions for tea lights made easy.

35. Easy Molded Candle

- 1lb/454g of melt point paraffin wax
- 0.16oz/4.5g of Vybar 103
- 1oz/28.3g of your choice of essential oils
- Wax dye of your color choice (optional)
- Glass containers
- Candle wicks

Method: Follow the instructions for making a simple molded candle.

Chapter 8- 6 Common Candle Making Errors

Using the same wick for every scent

Creating the perfect candle all comes down to using the correct wick. Creating a candle that smells great but is still safe to burn can be a challenging process for a beginner. This is because choosing the correct type and size can be a daunting process as there are various kinds to choose from. However, don't be swept up in the difficulty of things and use just any old wick because depending on the fragrance and amount used can also affect the performance of your candle in two separate ways. Either by altering the relationship with your wax or the amount of oil present in your candle. Every oil is different, and far too many candle makers disregard the importance of using the correct wick. Even if you have been successful in the past, once you begin changing your oils or amounts, you could very well run into problems that only a different wick type or size can resolve.

Using incorrect ingredients

You can find many candle tutorials online that include low-quality ingredients or materials. Using these inferior products or supplies, you risk exposing yourself to underperforming candles and potential fire hazards. So, don't use things such as food coloring, thin-walled glass containers, crayons, plastic containers, or excessive leaves or dried materials. Additionally, items such as glitter (which can be used albeit sparingly) and metal tins that aren't sealed are also items you shouldn't use.

Adding the incorrect amount of essential or fragrance oils

As a beginner to candle craft, you may be wondering just how much fragrance to use, so take this rule with you whenever you're in the mood for some candle making. The rule is as follows: 1lb/454g of wax per 1oz/28g of oil. Alternatively, you can also multiply 0.625 by the weight of your wax in either ounces or grams. Moreover, it is vital to remember to measure them by weight and not by volume when adding in any oils or wax.

Starting with too many materials

There are copious variations of wicks, waxes, containers, colors, molds, and essential and fragrance oils available, which can help you achieve your perfect candle. Moreover, as a novice to the craft, you may get overwhelmed with all the different options available, and it is not uncommon to forget that getting the first candle spot on is the first crucial step in the creation process.

You're more likely to have issues if you are constantly changing things up, so keep it simple as you start out, and as you become more confident, you will have plenty of opportunities to express your creativity. You can achieve this by simplifying the basic skills of the craft like testing and adjusting wick sizes, for example, into easier-to-understand terms, which will have you on your way to testing out new ideas in no time. Don't be fooled though, making candles is no easy task as your candle will need to meet the basics of safety and industry standards, especially if you want to create a business through candle making.

However, if you are simply doing this as a hobby or for fun and not as a business venture, you won't need to pay too much attention to industry regulations and safety standards. If you are, you will need to gather more information about your local safety and regulation standards in the areas you will sell or manufacture your candles.

Burning your candle before it has fully cured

As a candle maker, you will need to master patience because before you can burn any candle, it will need to be fully cured or set first. To simplify things, you can only gauge how a candle will burn once it has first been lit. In further detail, it is a bit more complex as wax contracts as a solid and expands as a liquid, and you may think that your candle has been set a few hours after pouring, but you would be mistaken. In reality, a candle can take as long as two weeks to set and cure completely before it can be burned.

Therefore by having a longer curing time, you will raise the amount of heat needed to melt the wax. What this means is if you burn a candle too soon after it has been poured, you could end up with a candle that has a strong scent, but the wick ultimately burns too hot. Therefore, waiting until your candles have fully cured before burning them is the best course of action and will allow your candle to burn just right.

Not doing a burn test and melt test

Testing your candles for safety is one of the most crucial steps in the candle-making process, and for your own safety and those around you, you should not take it lightly. By not performing a burn test, there is no way to know if your design is safe and will meet guidelines. Testing candles requires time and patience because you won't know it is safe until it either fails to meet your safety standard or is completely burned down.

To successfully establish an accurate burn test, you will need to repeat the process a few times because a candle can appear safe after the first burn, but you could run into some issues after the next. So for your safety and others, be sure to establish a routine and take notes whenever applicable. Moreover, it is vital to note that a melt pool is not a successful indicator as to whether a test was successful; this can only be seen through consecutive burn tests using both methods for indication.

Chapter 9- Diagnosing and Fixing Any Problems

Why is my candle changing color?

This is often caused when you add in your color, and your wax is too hot. To avoid candle color changes, it is best to keep the temperature of your wax under 190F/. Alternatively, some wax dyes are susceptible to color changes when exposed to direct sunlight or UV rays. You can take precautions to prevent this if you are willing to purchase additives for UV protection.

Why is my candle burning right down the center?

Typically a hard wax candle can burn right down the wick while the rest of the candle remains intact. Having a hole straight down the middle of your wax will cause the flame to be unable to continue burning. Using a softer wax container wax will have a better result; however, this can cause the wax to pool beneath the base of your candle. Specifically speaking, this is a common problem when making pillar candles, especially if you will be using wax with a lower melting point.

Why won't my candle burn?

This problem can be caused by an un-primed wick and can be easily resolved by lighting the candle upside down. This will allow the melted wax to run down onto the wick, subsequently coating or priming it, allowing the candle to light.

Why does my candle stop burning?

This is a common problem in candles with spices, essential oils, or colors that do not meet quality standards. As such, these inferior products can clog your wick, preventing it from burning.

Why is my candle's surface cracked?

This problem is often the result of cooling your candle too quickly or leaving it too long in the freezer. As such, try to keep a constant eye on your candle as it cools or sets in the freezer because you do not want to freeze your wax.

Why is there excess wax on my container walls?

A container candle that has only been lit for a period of fewer than four hours can result in excess unburned wax staining the inside of your container. This is because container candles are best suited for longer burns.

Why won't my candle release from its mold?

There can be a few particular causes for this problem, beginning with the type of wax you are using, particularly, beeswax which often produces a stickier candle that hardly shrinks during curing. This can result in the candle being difficult to release from its mold and, as such, is not advised for use in molded candles unless you are using a mold releaser.

Similarly, you can also have a damaged mold, which will also make the candle release difficult. As such, you can try placing your mold into the freezer for about 5-10 minutes or adding extra stearic acid into your wax solution. Alternatively, you can place your candles beneath some hot water to aid in mold release; however, this can cause deformities to appear on the exterior of your candle.

Why is my candle dripping?

A dripping candle can result from a wick that is too small and, as such, cannot absorb enough wax, or you are using the incorrect type of wick for the candle. Additionally, this problem can be caused by incorrect wick placement. Moreover, the wax used could have been too soft or had too low of a melting point. Alternatively, you could just be suffering from a strong breeze that is disrupting your flame.

Why does my candle have shrink wells?

This is a fairly common problem amongst blended paraffin wax as the wax cools and then shrinks, creating an indentation around the wick. You can resolve this by keeping your leftover wax to be re-melted and poured to fill in the cavity until it is level. Similarly, this problem can also occur at the base of your candle, but you can easily trim this to straighten out the candle. Afterward, you can use a frying pan lined with aluminum foil to flatten out the base of your candle so that it is uniform and even.

Alternatively, you can include a blend of 1 part beeswax to 4 parts paraffin wax to help to reduce the shrinkage of your candle. Bear in mind, however, that by using a beeswax and paraffin blend will require a bigger-sized wick. Moreover, you can also use a wax additive like Vybar to help to combat shrinkage, but this could affect the performance of your candle.

Why is the scent in my candles so weak?

When your candle loses its aroma, it can be because you added in your scent when your wax was too hot or you did not add in enough for the type of wax you are using. To avoid this problem, it is best to pour any scents into your melted wax at the very last minute in addition to adding your vybar, which should be used sparingly as large amounts can cause the molecules to bind, and therefore no scent will be released. It is important to note that some on-pour waxes already contain vybar, so be sure to read the label and manufacturer instructions.

Why have the sides of my candle sunken in?

Having the sides of your candle caving in can often result from air pockets that have become trapped within your candle. To avoid this problem, simply ensure that you gently tap the base of your mold or container to remove any lodged air bubbles that may be present within your candle.

Why is my flame weak or drowning?

If your flame is too weak or drowning, it could be because your wick is too short or loose. Additionally, it can also be because your wax melting point is too high for the size wick you are using. To lessen the probability of this problem arising in future batches, try adding in less stearic acid or other additives you may have used during manufacturing.

Why is my flame sputtering?

A sputtering flame could be the result of an open oil or air pocket within your candle. To lessen the probability of this occurring to your candles, it is best to tap the base of your container or mold to eliminate the trapped air or oil inside your wax. Additionally, if you have used a wet container to pour your wax, be advised that water drops can enter into your wax, forming a water pocket. To lessen the chance of this problem occurring, it is advised to dry off any utensils or equipment which could possibly come into contact with your wax.

Why is my candle molting or has a snowflake pattern?

A candle that is molting or has a snowflake pattern is typically the result of having poured your wax when it was too cold, or your candle hasn't cooled fast enough. Additionally, adding in too much stearic acid, palm wax, or essential oils can also have the same effect. This is why adding at most 1% vybar to reduce or possibly eliminate this error is recommended.

Why is my candle smoking?

This issue can result from a wick that is too thick, too long, or the wrong type for the wax you are using. Try trimming your wick to the advised ¼ of an inch/0.6cm long. Additionally, you will also need to check for any wind drafts around your flame to reduce or eliminate this issue.

Chapter 10- Decorating and Storing Your Candles

Decorating

Mixing colors and layering

To create new colors, you can always mix different wax dye colors together. Be sure that you are taking notes to record the amounts you have used to replicate them in the future. Adding layers to your candle is a creative way to add pops of color to your candle, but it will first take some practice. Layering colors takes time and patience as you will need the previous layer to be thoroughly cooled (no longer opaque) before you can begin pouring your second layer.

When pouring your layers, the temperature must be no higher than 140F/60C to guarantee that the colors don't melt into each other. You may lose some glass adhesion or experience frosting if you are waiting too long in-between pouring your layers, as this gives the wax time to lift from the glass.

Painting your candles

Steps

1. Before beginning, start by cleaning the surface of your candle using a small amount of rubbing alcohol to remove any dust. Now, slightly wet a lint-free cloth with a small amount of rubbing alcohol, then gently wipe the exterior of the candle to prepare for painting.
2. Next, you will need to apply a thin, even coat of candle varnish (which can be purchased at your local DIY or arts and crafts store) to your candle's surface. By varnishing the exterior of your candle, you will be protecting it from any damage while preparing the surface to allow the paint. Leave the varnish to dry overnight.

3. Your candle is ready for paint start by sectioning off any areas you don't want to get paint on using rubber bands or tape. If you are not set on painting your whole candle, you can simply add designs or stripes with painter's tape or rubber bands. To achieve this, you will need to press the tape or rubber bands flush to the candle's surface for better access while painting. A little tip if you place the tape all the way around the candle, you can create a complete striped design. Alternatively, if you wish to create more than one stripe, you can overlap tapes of different widths.
4. Next, using acrylic paint, you can start by painting your candle in even and distinct layers. If you are using different colors, it is best to paint all sections of the same color first before moving onto a different color. Alternatively, you can use separate bushes to paint different colors onto your candle. Just be sure to keep these with their appropriate colors or to clean them well before using a different color. Moreover, it would be advised to always cover your workstation with newspaper before you begin to prevent any spills from damaging your surface.
5. Lastly, set your candles aside to dry overnight, checking in the morning to see if you can see the candle through the paint. If so, you will need to add another coat and then leave it to dry again overnight. Once you are happy with your color, you can go ahead and apply an even coat of varnish over the entirety of your candle. By doing this, you are ultimately sealing the candle from becoming susceptible to cracks and chips forming on the surface of your paint which will, in turn, give your candle a glossy finish.

Decorating with glitter (in small amounts)

Steps

1. First, start by first placing tissue paper around the areas of your candle you don't want glitter. You can do this by taping strips of tissue paper or individual pieces to create designs.

It is crucial to always first plan out your design before taping it down with some scotch tape before you begin adding the glitter, as it cannot be removed once applied.
2. Next, begin covering the areas you want to place your glitter on by using a glue-like mod podge to paint a thin, even layer onto the candle. You can paint over your taped areas for full coverage, but try not to cover them entirely.
3. Now you can start sprinkling the glitter over the areas where you have applied the glue, considering that thick coats of glitter will look the best but will clog your wick, so use the glitter sparingly. Once covered, you shouldn't be able to see any of your candles beneath the surface. Remember to protect your workstation with paper so that you don't get glitter everywhere. Moreover, you will need to remove excess glitter by tapping the base gently against a surface.
4. Now you can let your candle dry overnight; the next day, you can remove any paper cutouts or designs before sealing the exterior with a mod podge sealer.

Decorating with images printed onto tissue paper

Steps

1. For this decorative method, you will first need to print an image onto a sheet of white or translucent tissue paper, just smaller than a standard printer sheet. Next, tape the tissue paper with the glossy side down onto a printer sheet and place it into the printer so that the image transfers onto the tissue paper. Remember that some printers will swap the paper over before printing, so be sure to check your printer's instructions before you begin. This transfer method will work well with illustrations, a few words, or even photos.
2. Next, cut out the image you have printed onto the tissue paper using scissors, be sure to leave a small border around the perimeter, as well as making sure that your image isn't too large to fit onto the side of your candle.

3. Now place your cut image onto the exterior of your candle, making sure it is flush with the surface on all sides before wrapping it with wax paper until your entire candle is covered completely. Be careful not to leave any creases or folds in your wax paper as you do this, as it could affect the transfer of the image onto the candle.
4. Once you are sure there are no creases in your wax paper, you can start applying heat using a heat gun or hairdryer to transfer the image over onto the candle. Remember to keep an eye on the ink as it is transferring because once the transfer is complete, you should be able to clearly see the ink coming through darker.
5. All that's left is to slowly and gently remove the wax paper from the sides of your candle. Do not rush, as you won't want the image to break while transferring. Once removed, you should have your own unique image decoration. Take note that this transfer method works best for lighter-colored candles, as you will appreciate the image more.

Embellishing candles using different items

This method of decoration has the most freedom when it comes to exterior design. Embellishing your candle can be done in dozens of ways, with only a few of them listed below. Keep in mind that using this method of decorating will yield the best results with plain candles. Additionally, most of these methods will require you to supervise your candle to trim away the decorative material not to create a fire hazard.

Wrapping your candles perimeter with cinnamon sticks

Steps

1. Wrapping the exterior of your candle with cinnamon sticks will give your candle a spic aroma and rustic look while it burns. Simply purchase enough cinnamon sticks to encircle the perimeter of your candle.

2. Next, place a small amount of heat-resistant glue to the back of each stick, placing each onto the exterior of your candle until fully wrapped.
3. Lastly, wrap a small ribbon or piece of string around the sticks and tie it off for decoration. Additionally, you can even add in a few bunches of cranberries or holly to complete the final look.

Using ribbons to incorporate flowers

Steps

1. For this option of decorating, simply wrap ribbon around the outside of your candle.
2. Next, add a real or fake flower and secure it with the ribbon to the exterior of your candle. You can even add extra ribbon to give your candle a more sophisticated appearance.
3. As your candle burns, you will need to cut the ribbon or flowers to prevent any fire hazard from occurring.

Decorating with beads, plastic jewels, or rhinestones.

Steps

1. Purchase beads, plastic jewels, or rhinestones from your local DIY or arts and crafts store.
2. Place your items in a design of matching colors or freely using a small amount of super glue to keep them in place. Alternatively, you can also purchase the rhinestones, which already have adhesive backs which you can stick directly to the sides of your candle.
3. Remember to keep an eye out while your candle burns to remove any decorative material before it comes into contact with your flame.

Decorating with sand and seashells

Steps

1. Gather some seashells (be sure to clean them before use) and sand from your local beach, DIY, or arts and crafts store.
2. Next, use a paintbrush with either liquid glue or mod podge to paint a small amount of glue onto the bottom ⅓/ or ½ of your candle.
3. Now roll the glued section of the candle throughout the beach sand until evenly distributed, then leave to dry overnight.
4. You can gently tap the candle to remove any loose bits of sand from the surface in the morning. Then you can stick or tie with yarn or string a few seashells or as much as you desire to the area above where the sand ends. Be advised that this method will work best with cream or plain colored candles.

Wrap the exterior of your candle with twine, fabric, or yarn.

Steps

1. Choose a yarn, ribbon, or fabric that will enhance the color of your candle.
2. Next, wrap your choice of twine, fabric, or ribbon around your candle to create the striped effect securing it to your candle with a small amount of mod podge or liquid glue. Alternatively, you can also wrap the candle diagonally across to give a new look to your candle. Remember to trim the fabric, yarn, or twine as you burn your candle to prevent any fire hazards.

Marbling and swirling

This technique is a bit more of a challenge, especially as a beginner, but like everything in life, you should get it in no time with a bit of practice. Marbling or swirling can produce an array of designs if you get the consistency of your wax right. This process gave the wax colors just enough time to melt together to create the swirled or marbled design, which works well in a mold.

Steps

1. For this technique, you can alternate each of your wax colors at 135F/57C, stopping for 1-3 minutes between each layer, as this will give your candle the best effect.

Storing candles safely

The importance of fire safety

As a potential fire hazard, candles should not be taken lightly and should be stored away from any pets or children even when they are not in use. Additionally, when storing candles, anything flammable such as cardboard, should be avoided to be on the safe side.

Avoid storing candles in high moisture areas

High moisture areas like under your sink or in your basement are not advised for storing candles. Candles require a dry environment where they won't come into contact with water and, as such, will be free from damage. However, you can store certain candles, such as jar candles in your basement as long as it is relatively dry and has a lid covering it.

Keep candles out of direct sunlight.

Sunlight can do more damage to your candles than simply telling them. The sun can alter the scent and the very color of your candle, making them fade faster due to the harmful UV rays. Meaning the darker the area you keep your candles, the longer they will last, especially if you are storing them properly.

Storing jar and tumble candles.

These types of candles, unlike the tapered or pillar variety, prefer to be stored upright. Container candles, as they are referred to, keep the wax from warping or melting and are easier to maintain than other candle varieties. Moreover, jar and container candles retain scents for longer, helping to give your candle a longer shelf life. Additionally, you can safely stack your unused containers or jars in a basket or box in the area you will be utilizing the most frequently. As a result, your jars and containers are out of the wax and protected from any unnecessary breaks, chips, or other damages.

Storing different candles

Tumblers, jars, and containers

As these types of candles generally come with their own container and or lid, you can store these candles as is without worrying about finding a specific container to put them in.

Pillar candles

For these kinds of candles, you will need to lay them on a flat surface as they will be less likely to bend, droop or warp when they are supported from beneath.

Taper candles

It would be best if you individually wrapped taper candles with tissue paper to prevent them from sticking together before putting them into storage. However, keep in mind that tissue paper is just as flammable as candles, so you will need to be careful how and where you store them.

Moreover, it would be best if you avoided piling or stacking long taper candles as their shapes make them slightly more fragile than standard candles.

Additionally, if you are overly concerned about wrapping your candles in tissue paper because of the fire hazard, you can opt for more natural and eco-friendly alternatives. Fabrics such as wool and silk are fire retardant and will be the safest to use to wrap and store your candles.

Scented candles

In order to keep your scented candles smelling as fresh as when you first made them, you will need to store them in either a sealable plastic or fabric bag. Alternatively, you can wrap parchment paper or plastic wrap around the candle as a last resort if you don't have a plastic or fabric bag on hand. Just be sure to secure them using tape or rubber bands so no scent can escape through the gaps.

Storing candles at room temperature

As the function of a candle is to be burned to provide light, luxury, or both, you don't want them to spoil when you are not around. As such, you should take caution against storing your candles in hot areas as anything above room temperature is likely to cause problems like bending, softening, or the complete melting of your candles. This problem is likely to occur with tapered or pillared candles, and as such, container candles will be immune to these effects.

Choosing the correct container to store your candles in

Metal

This is the best type of container to store your candles in because metal is impervious to fire, rot, and moisture. Moreover, metal is highly durable, and therefore you won't have to worry about your candles getting squashed or damaged.

Plastic

The main benefit of storing candles in plastic containers is the sheer amount of available sizes, in addition to being inexpensive and easily available. However, plastic containers are susceptible to heat, so be sure to store the container away from direct heat or in a room with a temperature below average.

<u>Cardboard</u>

This type of storage method should be your last resort when you are deciding what to store your candles in. But if you have no other choices, a plain and sturdy cardboard box in a dark, cool and dry area will work just fine at a push. However, if you can spend a bit on storage containers for your candles, both you and your candles will surely benefit.

Conclusion

To conclude, even though making candles can be a tricky process that requires a lot of time, patience, and dedication, it can also be a rewarding one full of fun, creativity, and exploration. By now, you should be confident that the basic skills of candle-making have been covered, and you can eagerly try out some new recipes all in the comfort of your own home with the new skills you have learned.

However, the extent of candle-making can only truly be expressed through experimentation and can only be appreciated once you get the hang of things. How far you take candle-making is up to you but remember that the sky's the limit and the possibilities are virtually endless, so go out and have fun. At the same time, you play around with aromas, blends, colors, shapes, and sizes, all to create a unique and personal candle just for you or for those you love.